Write

Out

Loud

A Compilation Of Poetic Works By

BRIDGET DAVIDSON

VENETIA JORDAN

DAWN ROSS

&

ALEXIS AUSTIN

HOOKED ON
BOOKS
PUBLICATIONS

Table of Contents

Foreword

This book is in celebration of four beautiful women. Each of us in our own unique way had something to say. Whether writing from love or pain, we wrote as a way to channel and express those emotions. At times we needed to shout, but felt no one was listening. We used a pen as the microphone, and the paper as our only audience. This book was a way of giving voice to those thoughts while we're still here and long after we've departed. For anyone who stumbles across the works within these pages, we hope you hear all the love, pain, heartbreak, and wisdom, and can appreciate what we have to say.

Alexis "Lexi" Austin

Enjoys nothing more than spending time with her son and watching him as he grows into his little personality. With Alexis what you see is what you get, she is very straight forward. If you ask her a question, be absolutely certain you *really* want to know the answer 'cause she is gonna give it to you straight, no chaser! Alexis is a quiet storm, but don't be fooled the lightning is always just below the surface.

I'm Down Bad

I'm down bad

It causes my thoughts to bleed and my pen these
words to leak.
I'm trying to see how this happened to me.
Is this scene real? Could this really be?
Is it a bad dream, or make believe?
I guess reality hits when I look down and see
her lying there and unable to breathe.
Her voice is now silent, no more words left to
speak.

I'm down bad

My thoughts are rewinding to where this road
led.
Hearing over and over all the things that she said.
All the drama and pain way too much for my
head.
Looking back I should have just walked away.
Just let her have him, not begged him to stay.

I'm down bad

They're coming now; I'll be soon locked away.
I can't keep from thinking what's he gonna say?
Will he visit me often or not even one day?

I'm down bad

Will he miss me immensely? Will he even be sad?
Will he grieve for her only, or miss the love that
we had?

I'm down bad

She's erased now from life I thought I'd be glad.
I'm standing here helpless and in shackles I'm
clad.
This thought comes to mind... I've lost all that I
had.

And all I can say is...

I'm down bad.

What Shall Become of the Rose

My heart is like a rose planted in the garden
of your soul.

Will you encourage me to blossom to my
full potential,
or pick me apart petal by petal until I have
no more of me to give?

Will you provide sunlight giving me the
encouragement I need to grow,
or cast a shadow, causing me to have self-doubt?

Will you feed my mind positive thoughts,
or will you offer only criticism and hurtful words?

Will you shower me with love
to keep me from emotionally wilting,
or will you deny me what I need
to thrive and watch me wither away?

If I give you this precious gift
What shall become of the Rose?

Written by Alexis Austin co – authored by Bridget
Davidson

Who's That Girl

Who is that girl hiding in the shadows?

Is she a girl lost in the cycle?
Or is she the ideal woman with her own
ideas about the world?

Is she this indescribable black diamond,
priceless, with a radiance that can't help but
attract?
Or just another flower in a garden full of
roses hoping to be picked?

Is she a talented female full of potential,
constantly reaching higher?
Or has she allowed fear to stifle her growth?

Is she a girl open and ready for love?
Or a girl that has given love until her heart aches?

Who is this girl?

Maybe no one will ever know or understand
because she is trapped in a box
that at times it seems no one can open
not even she

Venetia "V the Diva" Jordan

A mother of two and a Vee Vee to one. Venetia is an educator, a fearless leader and an extremely loyal friend. If someone she loves and cares about needs her she is there, no questions asked. She has a joyful and nurturing spirit and is very family oriented. Venetia loves to laugh and have a good time but beware if she goes silent what comes next will feel like darts, and you can best believe she won't miss!

Does She?

Does she
Rub your head till you fall asleep?
Know your words before you speak?
Compliment your style when you take her out?
Understand you as a man and know what you're
about?

Does she
Call or text when she enters your thoughts?
Take the time to listen when others will not?
Offer assistance with no second thought?

Does she
Ignite calming elements of peace because
your pain makes her blue?
Make your heart melt when she smiles at you?
Match each note of your love rhythm too?

NO, she doesn't
that's easy to see,
She doesn't; she couldn't
because she is not me.

I Used To...

I used to believe you would always be there,
until I realized you never really were.

I used to feel in my heart you were all mine,
until constant heartache proved that was all in
my mind.

I used to think the future looked bright,
until without a second thought,
you turned off the lights.

I used to believe the words you spoke,
until I realized actions speak the truth.

I used to be sure I could count on you,
until you abandoned me when I needed you
most.

I used to allow Us to be dominated by You,
until I realized the other half of We is Me.

I used to make you my priority,
until I realized I was just your option.

I used to....
until... now

Night Passes

Another night passes
I lie here with thoughts of you.
My face a constant in your memory
as you continue to seek
what I have already found.

As past turns to future,
need grows stronger as time goes by.
The haze slowly lifts and
the pathway becomes clear.

Your heart knows the way home
my glow is your guiding light.
Another night passes
I lie here at last with...
You

Twin Souls

We are twin souls that met in passing
both searching for true love that's everlasting.
We threw our hearts out there over and over
but that connection elusive as a four-leaf clover.
The years went by, and we just couldn't shake it
If we tried it again,
this time could we make it?
The feelings we have are so strong
if we work really hard, can we both hold on?
After all, we are just
twin souls who met in passing...

Dawn "D Stylz" Ross

A lover of music and spoken word poetry. When life permits, she enjoys vacationing near a beautiful body of water and lounging on the beach. Dawn loves attending concerts and comedy shows. When she has time to relax you can find her curled up with a good book. She enjoys spending time with her family and absolutely adores her son.

Head to Toe

As endearing as a kiss on the forehead
As loving as a kiss on the cheek

As passionate as a kiss on the lips
Your actions are making me weak

As seductive as a kiss on the collarbone
As sexy as a kiss on the breast

As hot as a kiss on the belly
I'm craving your sweet caress

As sensual as a kiss on the thigh
As playful as a kiss on the knee

As erotic as a kiss on the feet
You have brought me to ecstasy

Innocent Pleasure

Countless conversations of intimate interludes
Saying enough to arouse sensual pleasure,
Yet allowing nature to maintain her peace.
Indulging in another innocent pleasure
That leaves long lasting smiles well after the
conversations ease.

No Shades of Grey

Close your eyes.
Try to see past
the fullness of my lips
the sway in my back
and the curve in my hips.
Open your heart.
Do not judge me by
the stature of my frame
whether big or small
short, average, or tall.
Maybe then we could have a conversation,
and you will not only hear me when I speak
but really listen to what I am saying.

The Forgettable Me

Who am I?

I was once your calm in the midst of storms, your peace when surrounded by chaos.

Laying your head on my chest to hear and feel my heartbeat was where you came to get yourself back in rhythm.

Breathing one another's air gave us life if we began to feel we were slipping away.

Touching fingertips and foreheads gave us the strength we needed when there was nothing more to give.

Our embrace intertwined us and sealed our love, and we vowed to unite for a lifetime.

However, somewhere along our journey,
time became a factor, and space became our
big divide.

Now I'm drifting on a memory so far
removed from you.

I barely get honorable mention, if I'm even
mentioned at all.

Who am I?

The Forgettable Me.

I Should Have Said No

I agreed to the friendship because I was sure
that once I heard your story it would be nothing
more.
You, however, had a very different plan
in spite of the agreement,
you were determined to become my man.
We were childhood acquaintances so I didn't
see the harm,
but I wasn't prepared for all of your charm.
I said no, you insisted,
I rejected, you persisted,
you were wearing me down
even though I resisted.
My resilience was getting weak,
I was caught off guard
and before I knew it you had my heart.
We've laughed, cried and shared future
endeavors.
you said with me you'd like a couple of forever's.
I ask how can that happen when you're already
involved?

Your response, "Just give me time, it will all be
resolved."
Years have gone by and nothing has changed,
yet you ask me to hang on because of benefits
you gain.
When it's all said and done
I 'll be the one to let go,
because from the very beginning
I should have said "NO!"

Troubled Man

I felt your pain today, and I cannot tell you why.
It pierced my soul so deeply, all I could do was
cry.
I cried tears of pain and sorrow as you so often
do,
I was overwhelmed by emotion
and felt deep compassion for you.
The troubles of the world rest heavily on your
mind.
Babies killing babies, folks going crazy, brothers
and sisters doing time.
You pace the floor at night and rock yourself to
sleep;
You pray to God Almighty that your soul He
surely keeps.
Mothers are getting younger, raising children all
alone.
It pains you to see them struggle,
trying to make it on their own.
Absent fathers offer no support
or even lend a hand.
You pray and plead with God
to help you understand.

Brothers out on corners hustle to make some ends.
Selling weed and crack to anyone,
including family and friends.
If they should die before they wake, who pays for their sins?
You're saddened by the reality that no one ever wins.
I felt your pain today, and now I do know why.
I, too am troubled by these things;
that's the reason that I cry
I pray we come together and formulate a plan,
to let this generation know we truly understand.
We've enabled our own destruction yet shocked we're taking the fall.
Let's find a real solution that benefits us all.

Sista, Sista

The most beautiful relationship I have is the
one I share with my sisters.

The schoolbooks, the Barbie's, the b-ball,
the boys

Football games, parties, and movies galore

"That's my shirt; give that back"
"I know you wore my shoes"
"She pulled my hair"
"You tattletale!"

Givin' each other the blues

We argue, we make up

We laugh, and we cry

We fight with each other
but that's the tie that binds

Disrespect one
then all you offend

Don't mess with this crew
or we will apprehend

The scholar, the queen, the tomboy, the diva

The creator, the writer, the soldier, the singa'

The paths we took that guided who we
came to be

never fail to lead us home
if there is a need

The sister bond is timeless
a circle that never ends

I love my girl's forever
my dearest trusted friends

Written by Dawn Ross co – authored by Bridget
Davidson

Bridget "Lady B" Davidson

Wife, mother, GiGi, sister, daughter, friend; Bridget has many hats, and she wears them all with style and grace. A very creative and introspective person that loves to spend her quiet time writing, making various projects, watching movies or getting lost in a good book. What Bridget cherishes most is spending time with family. She is one ferocious mama bear when it comes to her children and grands and she says quality time with the hubby lifts her spirits and soothes her soul.

Amorous Encounter

I don't mean to sound bold,
but I've been told
you have to ask for what you want.
Since we met, I've wanted to express
a proposition I'd like to suggest.
To use a phrase from Marvin Gaye
I will take a chance and simply say
Let's get it on

Don't let my words shock you.
You think I'm moving too fast?
I have to presume that you misunderstand,
before I caress you with the touch of my hand
I want to seduce you mentally.

Let me whisper in your ear, allowing me to
massage your mind,
then penetrate your cerebrum
giving you waves of intellectual orgasms
that will send spasms
all through your cranium.
I want more than just your body,
I need to feel your soul.
Hydrate the deep levels of your perception.
Expand and challenge your thoughts from
inception.

Allow us to be entwined
with foreplay of the mental kind.
I assure you the satisfaction of this mental
encounter will last longer,
and as the gratification of awareness gets
stronger,
we will succumb to the bliss of insight
and bask in the afterglow of a deeper
connection.

Is your intellect aroused enough to pursue
a tryst of minds between us two?
Amorous Encounter before physical affection.
We can do this in stages, not only one session.

An intimate start before the part
when our clothes are removed.

I need to be certain you're not confused,
Let me clear any doubt obstructing your view
Say just what I mean, not just a clue

I want to get it on... with you.

Attitude Adjustment

I am not the same girl I used to be.
I have said my farewells to the things and
people that bring nothing but negativity.
Gone are the days that I would suffer in
silence when I was mistreated,
now I speak my truth.
In expressing my truth, you may disagree,
but I leave no room to argue.
I say my piece, and then choose to be
silent, I have nothing to prove.
With maturity, I have learned that some
situations and circumstances
don't deserve my time, energy, or attention.
Not to mention I have no inclination to
entertain others' misery.

I can't help you carry that bag
ooops, I'm sorry, I lied,
the new me can be honest.
I could assist; I just choose not to.
I'm too busy taking out my own trash.
Difference is I'm dumping mine.
You choose to carry yours with you,
then complain that it's still there.

Once I cleaned out my closet and sorted
through the clutter, I realized
I didn't have even one dress to
wear to your pity party.

I am high styling, high stepping down this
new path that has been revealed to me.
Some will choose to come along,
others I left where they chose to be.
No time to waste or tears to shed
on those that are now history.
I'm easing on down the road to my destiny.
Get it right or get left behind that's my new
philosophy.

I'm still me just new and improved.
Look closely, and you'll see
a confident grown woman
not the girl I used to be.

Essence of PEACE

P is for the Privilege of receiving your Love and giving my Love to you

E is for the Ease your Love gives my soul

A is for the Absolute confidence that you will be there for me

C is for the Calm that comes over me when thoughts of you enter my mind

E is for Everything you have added to my life

PEACE
is the gift you have given to me

Fortified

Take my hand when you feel strong
for together, we are an unstoppable force

Take my hand when your spirit is weak
and I will motivate and encourage you

Take my hand in joyous times
for I will celebrate with you

Take my hand in times of sorrow
and we will cry together

Take my hand in triumph
as your victories are also mine

Take my hand when there is disappointment
and together, we will rebuild

Take my hand in prayer
for with God, all things are possible

Take my hand...
In Love

Give It Back

I stopped by today
to ask for my heart back
You see, there is someone worthy out there
that I may want to give it to

We had what we had
and we agreed no strings attached,
but somehow, you managed
to tie one around me
when I wasn't looking

Yeah, I knew
there were others pulling at you,
but since we had what we had
I was sure I could win
this tug-of-war

But the light finally came on
and now I see that
this string that had my heart so completely
bound had nothing on the other end

I gave my heart freely
you played with it

I trusted you with it
you broke it

So, please....
just give it back

I'll dust it off
put the pieces back together,
make it ready for someone deserving

Until then
I can hold onto it myself

Journey of Self Discovery

I used to be in such a hurry
never taking the time to look into
the mirror of my life
running past quickly
trying to avoid catching even a glimpse
of the Me that used to be

my subconscious screamed
"don't look, turn away"
I knew there was nothing but pain and sorrow
there

but then, a sudden turn of events
caused my perceived perfect world to shatter
and I had no choice but to slow down and take a
look

just as I feared,
there were
dilemmas from indiscretion

but working through those bad decisions
gave me wisdom

there was...

heart break from past loves

but those heartbreaks helped me make better
choices

sorrow from the loss of loved ones
but those losses taught me that life is precious

despair from life plans that didn't come to pass
but that despair taught me to handle
disappointment

trials I had to endure
but those trials made me stronger

I even saw naiveté
and although an accepted affliction of youth
still a trait considered undesirable once of
age

however, life experience has helped me mature
and the deeper I looked, the more it became
clear that the Me that used to be formed the
foundation of the Me that came to be

I am the sum of all of my life events
and I wouldn't change a thing

I no longer avoid looking
into the mirror of my life
I often stop and really take notice
of the strong, independent, empowered,
beautiful woman I am today...
and I smile

Love Unaware

There is a man which I have not met, but our
hearts are very familiar.

He knows my feelings, my laughter, my tears...
but his Love is unaware.

I know his strength, his courage, his love of God,
but my Love is unaware.

In search of Love, I walk east.
I see many men with handsome faces, chiseled
bodies, and lavish possessions.

On the same quest, he walks west; he sees many
women with hypnotic eyes, alluring breasts, and
tempting backsides.

We both lift our eyes to the heavens and pray,
"Dear Lord, please bring to light the one true
Love you have chosen just for me."

While in prayer, our paths cross.
We share a look, a smile, a nod of hello,
but then we both continue on our separate
ways,
our Love still unaware.

As if guided by more than just his will
this man slowly turns in my direction.

I am now far in the distance but he finally sees
me clearly.

He begins to walk slowly, then hastens
in my direction with the key to my heart in his
hand.

I allow him to unlock my heart and release
all the Love inside that is now fully aware

Magnetic

Your teasing advances
My playful protests

Your warm embrace
My cool attitude

Your alluring hands busy
My body relaxing

Your desire growing
My resistance shrinking

Our clothes disappearing
Our bodies uniting

My door to love yearning
You're there with the key

My breathing sporadic
Your rhythm increasing

My plentiful kisses
Your hungry acceptance

My words of love whispered
You're yelling my name

Our moment arriving
Our finale tremendous

My mind reflecting
Your body sleeping

My teasing advances...

Present State of Mind

I Am...
longing for you
dreaming of the last time that we...
rewinding in my mind's eye that beautiful,
passionate encounter
pausing on the most sensual scenes

I Am...
craving your touch
imagining your hands caressing every inch
of me
filled with desire
unable to stop these images that are
traveling from my mind to areas southward

I Am...
now fully awake
engulfed in desire
reaching for you in the dark
coaxing you into my fantasy

I Am...
so happy that you are here, and mine
intoxicated with our lust
overtaken by love
completely satisfied

Quick Lesson in Math

$1 + 1 = 2$

1 man
+
1 woman
_____
= 2 individuals

We women, tend to forget that "1" is a
whole number, not a fraction.
So, we sometimes
add a man who
divides our legs
subtracts our self-worth
and,
multiplies our pain.
The sum of this,
equals misery.
This leaves us feeling we are only a fraction
of our whole being.

The calculation of this equation often leads
to confusion until we realize,
the (square) root of the problem began with
the initial addition and subsequent division.
Ladies, the addition of a partner is not to
reduce OR complete but to enhance.
So, it's time we learn the new math...
If a man does not add something to your life,
he should quickly be subtracted from the
equation and...
I promise your self-worth will multiply.

Too Much

He said: I think we should take a break

She said: Break?
He said: This is getting way too heavy
She said: Heavy?
He said: Yes, This relationship stuff... it's
just too much.

She pauses before she replies,
really pondering on what could be so heavy
and just too much for this man.

After much reflection
on the relationship and what each
of them has brought to the table she said:
I think you're right; I am too much
for you

I am
Too intelligent
Too beautiful
Too strong

And way too tired to hold onto anything you are
trying to give me that makes me feel I am not
enough.

I am a queen, and I cannot and will not
remove any jewels from my crown
to make it easier for you to carry

I need a king that is strong enough to
wear his crown and help make sure mine shines
and stays intact

He said: nothing. Only watched with regret
as she adjusted her crown and walked out of
his life.

Unfinished

I am a work in progress
Forever learning and growing
Making myself over
Making myself better
Becoming a greater... Me

Gaining knowledge from books, experience,
observation
and from others who have walked this walk
before me
Gaining strength from disappointment, trials,
struggles and heartbreak

That bag of misery and bitterness you tried to
give me
I said no thanks
and left it right there at your place
I decided I had no room at all for that in my
space
Instead, I took an armful of strength and
lessons learned and added those to the box I
started long ago

Every time I look at it...look in it, shake it
up and rearrange it, I am reminded that I can
indeed, get up, move on, and push through
Because I am constantly evolving

You thought since I was unfinished,
I would come undone
Never that
My foundation is too solid
My spirit, my stride, my strength
is not easily broken

Will this project ever be completed?
I hope not
I want to go from good to better
From better to best
From best to... beyond my wildest dreams
I want to be the greatest Me that I can be

But as with all projects, mine too will
someday come to an end
(But only when there is no more breath left
in me)
Until then
I am a work in progress

Watch This

I am watching you, watching me.

I became accustomed to seeing me through
your eyes.
Do you think I'm pretty? Are you enticed by my
charm?
Or do my flaws overshadow all that could be
appealing, making me an insignificant part of
the crowd?

I don't profess to be the prettiest, most alluring
or best dressed
I am one spectacular, beautiful mess.

Ordinary
That was your view, and you almost made me
believe it too.
But there are so many facets of me, I am a
chameleon.
At any given time, I may be
happy, sad, reflective, pissed off, inspired,
confident, frantic, crazy...
Any or all of that and more
as I am constantly changing, evolving, growing,

and you're in the background, watching.

I don't bring my representative, fired her a
looong time ago.
I don't have the energy, inclination, or the will
power for pretending to be someone else.
I work too hard at being the most exceptional...
Me.
I've made some bad decisions but I have no
regrets.
My journey needed every hill and valley to bring
me here, and I am better than just all right.
Still, you're watching.

In your eyes I am merely pieces, parts, and
fragments.
You pick me apart, separating the things you
deem as "good"
But I am whole, complete, and intact without
your approval.

Under your glare, it was dark. I was sad,
insecure, uncertain.
But finally the light came on, and I began to see
things clearly.
I put in the work to make some changes.

Gone is the time my thoughts are silenced.
Now things I once tolerated I say out loud they
are intolerable and I won't participate.
Now I speak my truth.
I am unapologetically me!

This transformation came while you were
watching.
I am now happy, blessed, at peace,
not because of you but in spite of.

Yes, you were always watching, but you never
really saw me.
You are now in my rearview
and I'm watching you
while you're watching me...
as I move on without you.

Afterword

This book was truly a labor of love. My sisters, my niece, and I have been writing poetry for years for our own enjoyment and sometimes as a means of self-therapy. We had each been told individually, by those granted the privilege of having a peek inside our thoughts, that our writing deserved a place to be heard but none of us ever really thought anything of it. We jokingly tossed the idea around a few times over the years but finally, after being poked, and prodded, we were finally convinced to release our musings. Our styles are very different as we are all speaking our own truth. Every passage from every poem was written from the heart. We sincerely hope within these pages you find that some (or all) of our pieces speak to you in some way, and you enjoy reading them as much as we enjoy bringing them to you.

CPSIA information can be obtained
at www.ICGtesting.com
Printed in the USA
LVHW071025051122
732438LV00024B/1507

9 781088 068922